Asombrosos anim

MOSCAS

By BrayJacobson
Traducido por Diana Osorio

Gareth Stevens
PUBLISHING

Please visit our website, www.garethstevens.com. For a free color catalog of all our high-quality books, call toll free 1-800-542-2595 or fax 1-877-542-2596.

Library of Congress Cataloging-in-Publication Data
Names: Jacobson, Bray, author.
Title: Moscas / Bray Jacobson.
Description: New York : Gareth Stevens Publishing, [2022] | Series: Asombrosos
   animalitos | Includes index.
Identifiers: LCCN 2020008133 | ISBN 9781538269190 (library binding) | ISBN
   9781538269176 (paperback) | ISBN 9781538269183 (6 Pack) | ISBN 9781538269206 (ebook)
Subjects: LCSH: Flies–Juvenile literature.
Classification: LCC QL533.2 .J33 2022 | DDC 595.7/35–dc23
LC record available at https://lccn.loc.gov/2020008133

First Edition

Published in 2022 by
Gareth Stevens Publishing
111 East 14th Street, Suite 349
New York, NY 10003

Translator: Diana Osorio
Editor, Spanish: Rossana Zúñiga
Designer: Katelyn E. Reynolds

Photo credits: Cover, p. 1 MR.AUKID PHUMSIRICHAT/Shutterstock.com; p. 5 Arterra/Universal Images Group via Getty Images; pp. 7, 24 (eggs) lensblur/ iStock / Getty Images Plus; pp. 9, 24 (larva) Gustavo Mazzarollo/ Moment / Getty Images Plus; p. 11 Goran Safarek / EyeEm/Getty Images; p. 13 Anthony Bannister/ Gallo Images / Getty Images Plus; pp. 15, 24 (pupa) George D. Lepp/ Corbis Documentary/Getty Images; p. 17 BirdShutterB/ iStock / Getty Images Plus; p. 19 Luis Castaneda Inc./ The Image Bank / Getty Images Plus; p. 21 Roel_Meijer/ iStock / Getty Images Plus; p. 23 Photographed and edited by Janos Csongor Kerekes/ Moment/Getty Images.

Printed in the United States of America

Some of the images in this book illustrate individuals who are models. The depictions do not imply actual situations or events.

CPSIA compliance information: Batch #CSGS22: For further information contact Gareth Stevens, New York, New York at 1-800-542-2595.

Find us on

Contenido

Las moscas viven en todo el mundo.
Existen muchas especies.

Las moscas ponen huevos.
¡Pueden haber
cientos de ellos!

Las larvas salen de
los huevos.
Parecen gusanos.

Les gustan
los lugares húmedos.

Comen mucho.
Crecen y mudan de piel.

Descansan como pupas.
Sus cuerpos cambian.

15

Todas las moscas
adultas tienen alas.
Tienen tres pares de patas.

Salen durante el día.

La mayoría
obtiene sus alimentos
de las flores.

¡Algunas moscas pican!

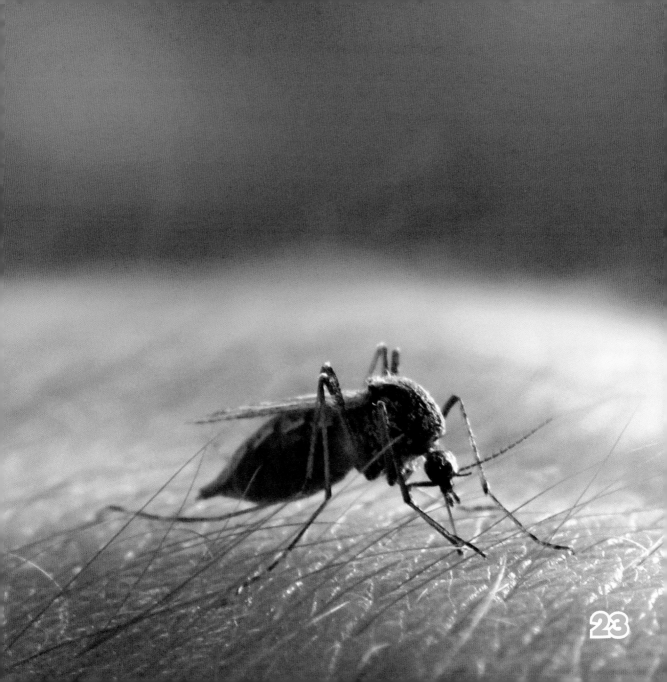

Palabras que debes aprender

huevos

larva

pupa

Índice